THE LITTLE BOOK OF
WITCHCRAFT

THE LITTLE BOOK OF WITCHCRAFT

Andrews McMeel Publishing
a division of Andrews McMeel Universal
1130 Walnut Street, Kansas City, Missouri 64106

www.andrewsmcmeel.com

First published in 2017 by Summersdale Publishers Ltd.
46 West Street,
Chichester, West Sussex
PO19 1RP, UK.

19 20 21 22 23 RLP 10 9 8 7 6 5 4 3

ISBN: 978-1-4494-9258-8

Library of Congress Control Number: 2017950660

Text: Anna Martin
Editor: Jean Z. Lucas
Art Director: Diane Marsh
Production Manager: Tamara Haus
Production Editor: Maureen Sullivan

ATTENTION: SCHOOLS AND BUSINESSES
Andrews McMeel books are available at quantity discounts with bulk
purchase for educational, business, or sales promotional use. For
information, please e-mail the Andrews McMeel Publishing Special
Sales Department: specialsales@amuniversal.com.

THE LITTLE BOOK OF
WITCHCRAFT

Andrews McMeel
PUBLISHING®

CONTENTS

Witchcraft was hung, in History, But History and I Find all the Witchcraft that we need Around us, every Day.

Emily Dickinson

INTRODUCTION

What does witchcraft make you think of? For many, it's the idea of ancient hags on broomsticks that fill the skies on Halloween night. For others, it's the witches in classical literature, such as the weird sisters in *Macbeth* and Morgan le Fay from Arthurian legend, while to a younger audience it's the boy wizard Harry Potter, who made magic something fascinating but eminently dark and not to be meddled with unless you've done your time at Hogwarts.

For those who have delved into the history of witchcraft, it's the notorious witch trials that are engraved on the memory. With these references, it's not so surprising that witchcraft is considered something dangerous and forbidden. Yet modern-day witchcraft, white witchcraft in particular, is altogether more palatable and accessible. Its focus is on using magic for positive purposes, and in a contemporary context this can mean anything from aiding the pursuit of love to unifying people who don't see eye to eye to even something mundane like assistance in finding the money to pay for an unexpectedly large water bill.

This book focuses on white witchcraft and the belief that all nature is magical. White witchcraft harnesses nature's power with the help of natural resources, such as crystals, herbs, and the phases of the moon, along with items traditionally associated with witchcraft, such as a wand or cauldron to perform spells and rituals. However, it's important to remember that the power of the mind is the most important tool in spell-casting.

The Little Book of Witchcraft will furnish you with knowledge as to the origins and possibilities of witchcraft; and, for those whose interest has been piqued, there is an introduction to casting spells and performing rituals for the twenty-first-century witch.

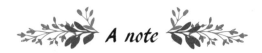

A note

Witchcraft is frequently considered the domain of women, but men and those who are gender fluid may also find that witchcraft resonates for them too.

ALL ABOUT WHITE WITCHCRAFT

White witchcraft in a nutshell

White witchcraft has a close association with paganism in its appreciation and worship of the natural world. By attuning into the forces of the earth, white witches believe they can bring luck to themselves and others; they can fulfill lifetime goals and attract love, good health, success, and happiness.

Those who perform white witchcraft believe that magic is within us all and that it is our birthright to reconnect with this power and learn how to harness it into spells and rituals for the purposes of good. The basic tools for white witchcraft are elements from nature, such as herbs, flowers, trees, and crystals, as well as the phases of the moon, the seasons, and sunlight. These are manipulated and combined with powerful words and actions to produce magic.

White witchcraft is a combination of mental, mystical, and spiritual practices—those who practice it believe that the human mind has the power to affect the world around them, as well as empowering them to take control of their own lives. The belief that the power of the mind enables the spell is akin to the principles of transcendental meditation, where a deep meditative trancelike state is achieved by clearing the mind and focusing on a mantra or image.

A word of warning—what goes around comes around

Witches can appear good or dark; however, those who perform white witchcraft believe in karmic law, and so the craft is never used for evil purposes. What is sent out will return to you threefold, which means the bad luck you cast will be three times worse for you when it comes back, so be careful!

WHITE WITCHCRAFT AND ITS RELEVANCE TODAY

Chances are if you have picked up this book you have more than a passing interest in witchcraft. Maybe you have always been interested in the magical realm. But it's not all dancing under a full moon and casting love spells. White witchcraft echoes modern society's views on the environment—the desire to nurture and protect the natural world—and resonates with modern self-help techniques, such as mindfulness and focusing on self-improvement to attain personal and professional goals. It's also about serving a greater good and nourishing the world and the people within it, and there is a healthy dose of feminism intrinsic to the practice too—with its celebration of the equality of the sexes and a woman's inner power. See—it's not just a load of hocus pocus! And that's the reason why many educated, intelligent people are swelling the ranks of those who practice witchcraft today.

Witchcraft permeates everyday life. Think of superstitions: how often do you knock on wood so as not to jinx something you've just said, or throw salt over your shoulder to get the devil in the eye? These actions are actually spells to prevent bad luck.

It's unclear how many practicing witches there are today, but over fifty-three thousand pagans were recorded in the UK census in 2011, and around two million in the United States. According to a 2016 report in the *Daily Mail*, educated career women are showing the most interest in witchcraft. Practicing magic is akin to mindfulness, making affirmations, and other forms of positive thinking and meditation, as it focuses the mind into experiencing the moment and reaching mentally for your goals, just with a few extra props, such as crystals, colored candles, and sometimes an altar or wand.

WHAT DOES A TWENTY-FIRST-CENTURY WITCH LOOK LIKE?

You're unlikely to spot a witch if you see one walking down the street, because they don't look like a Dürer engraving or Disney's Maleficent—they're more likely to be wearing a business suit and juggling a challenging job and family responsibilities. Modern witches tend not to advertise their calling, but there are subtle signs to look out for, such as a pentacle or ankh around their neck (you will learn more about these in the Signs and Symbols in Witchcraft section, page 59) or, if you stop by the home of a witch, you might see the tools for witchcraft, such as crystals clustered on a windowsill, or notice the smell of incense permeating the air. Many witches practice alone, but covens are still in existence. The idea of a coven of witches may give you visions of the weird sisters in *Macbeth*, but, in reality, modern-day witches like to meet up for a chat and share ideas just as much as anyone else. Although it can be rare to find like-minded people in the local community or among friends, today there are online, or virtual, covens where white witches swap their stories and cast spells.

SIGNS THAT YOU MIGHT BE A WITCH

Most people have an inkling that they might have a natural affinity for witchcraft—see if any of these statements apply to you:

★ You are attracted to the mystical and are sensitive to the energies of nature.

★ You are deeply curious about the universe and its undiscovered mysteries.

★ Your intuition tends to be spot on.

★ You feel a sense of your own personal power and strength.

★ You are fascinated by the mysteries of life and what might be beyond it.

★ You are sensitive to the changes in weather—you revel in the power of a storm.

★ Animals are attracted to you—cats and dogs follow you home.

★ You have an interest and a natural aptitude for healing.

★ You feel somehow different from your friends and family.

A BRIEF HISTORY OF WITCHCRAFT

Popular opinion of witchcraft is still very much rooted in stories of black magic and historical evidence of persecution. Famous witch trials from history—such as the Pendle trials in the early seventeenth century—live long in the public's consciousness. In order to understand witchcraft and what it means to be a witch, we need to consider its origins and connotations—both good and bad. Much of white witchcraft is rooted in the pagan practice known as Wicca. The origins of witchcraft are in no way easy to unpick, but we can begin by looking at Wicca and a timeline of witchcraft being practiced in Europe.

WICCA IN A NUTSHELL

Wicca, also known as green magic, is often seen as interchangeable with white witchcraft, but, while they hold many similarities in their worship of the natural world, they are not the same thing. Wicca is a pagan religion, albeit a modern one, whereas white witchcraft is not. "Pagan" is an old term for a country person, but in a modern context it refers to a follower of the cycles of the seasons and the movements of the sun and moon. The word "Wicca" comes from the Anglo-Saxon *wicce*, meaning wise, and the English word "witch" is derived from "Wicca."

Wicca promotes an appreciation of nature, acknowledging the seasons, the phases of the moon, the cycles of the sun, and the rhythm of nature, respecting all life. Its origins are pre-Christian, although much of its received wisdom is from more recent archaeological discoveries; there isn't much written evidence because the Christian church pilloried witches. The church portrayed witches as evil despite the majority using their skills for good, predominantly healing. Wiccans and witches do not worship Satan or summon demons and they do not promote cult behavior—there is no enforced coercion, and they never sacrifice living creatures or cause harm to others or possess any desire to denounce other religions.

The first Wiccans followed the teachings of Gerald Gardner, a nineteenth-century British academic and scholar, who revived the pagan traditions of working with nature, using herbs, essences, and other natural elements for healing, and brought it to public attention with a series of books, the most notable being *Witchcraft Today* in 1954. He also founded the Museum of Witchcraft and Magic in Boscastle, Cornwall.

Many modern witches prefer to be called Wiccans to escape the negative connotations of being called a witch. Wicca today blends well with modern holistic well-being practices, such as reiki, meditation, and aromatherapy, as well as spiritual interests, such as astrology and clairvoyance.

Angelic Wicca

Some Wiccans believe that angels help with their practices. Angels are prevalent in Christian and other religious faiths, but the angels that support Angelic Wicca are celestial beings made of love and light that are called upon as either guardians or mentors.

A TIMELINE OF WITCHCRAFT IN EUROPE

 12,000 years BC—There are cave paintings in southern France from the Palaeolithic period depicting a man with a stag's head and a pregnant woman standing in a circle with eleven other figures. This is believed to be one of the earliest depictions of witchcraft. Experts have deduced that these images represent Palaeolithic man's worship of nature as gods and goddesses—the horned god had supremacy over all animals, and pregnant women were recognized and revered as the creators of life. It's no accident that the Christian church redefined the horned man as the Devil, thus outlawing and demonizing these witchcraft rituals as devil worship.

 Circa 750–650 BC—In Homer's *Odyssey*, an enchantress called Circe turned people into pigs.

 Circa 630–540 BC—Witchcraft is condemned in the Old Testament. Witches appear in the Bible when King Saul seeks communion with the witch of Endor.

 Circa 420 BC—St. Augustine of Hippo dismisses witchcraft as the "error of pagans." According to

his view, witchcraft was relatively harmless and therefore witches were free from persecution. This view continued to hold sway in the late medieval Christian church.

 1208—Pope Innocent III publicly criticized those who claimed that both God and Satan had supernatural powers. Satan became feared, and attacks on witches increased as they were accused of worshipping dark forces.

 1273—Thomas Aquinas, a Dominican monk, declared that demons existed and that they could tempt people into performing acts of evil. Those who practiced witchcraft became widely feared.

 1400s—Witch trials became more prevalent across Europe. The accused were brought to trial over claims of transforming into animals, spreading evil curses and plagues, causing bad weather to ruin crops, and flying on broomsticks, among other crimes.

 1484—Pope Innocent VIII ordered a full report on suspected witchcraft practices, resulting in the publication of *Malleus Maleficarum*, which translates as "Hammer of Witches." This document became the definitive basis for determining a witch in a trial and led to many being prosecuted and executed.

1500s—Renaissance artists, such as Albrecht Dürer, recorded images of vile crones with hooked noses, which went a long way toward influencing the classical view of witches right up until the present day.

Mid-1500s to mid-1600s—Witch trials erupted en masse across Europe. Over a 150-year period, approximately 80,000 witches were executed. The biggest concentration was in Germany, where 26,000 witches were killed. Over 80 percent of these were women.

1563—The Witchcraft Act was introduced, which punished those who practiced witchcraft or consulted witches. Many people sought the services of witches, be it for health concerns or clairvoyance, but the church felt compromised, denouncing witchcraft as the work of the Devil. Most of the witches were old women whose appearances matched Dürer's caricatures, and they were also often poor. If they owned a cat, this was regarded as further evidence that they were a witch.

1590—King James VI of Scotland (who would later become King James I of England) and his new wife were caught up in a violent storm, which their captain blamed on witchcraft. Six witches admitted to the offense of causing the storm and were burned at the stake. The king didn't stop there, authorizing the torture and execution of suspected witches across Scotland in what became the biggest witch hunt in British history. He also wrote a book, *Daemonologie*, published in 1597, about his opposition to witchcraft and magical practices, which is believed to have directly influenced Shakespeare's *Macbeth*.

1606—*Macbeth* by William Shakespeare was performed for the first time. Its famous opening, showing three witches in a storm—*When shall we three meet again? / In thunder, lightning, or in rain? / When the hurlyburly's done, / When the battle's lost and won.*—indicates how widespread public interest in witchcraft was at this time.

1612—The Pendle witch trials took place when whole swaths of Lancashire, England, were reportedly suffering from the ill effects of witchcraft—no village was considered safe from dark magic. If sickness was to befall a family, they believed it was caused by a curse, and a poor harvest was often deemed the result of a bad wish.

 Early to mid-1640s—Following on from the mass witch hunts in Britain, France followed suit to conduct its own largest witch hunt in history with over 600 arrests.

 1645—East Anglia was gripped by witch fever. A man called Matthew Hopkins became Witchfinder General and was tasked with seeking out all forms of heresy and witchcraft, though his deductions were based on "witches' marks," such as a hairy wart or large mole on the suspect's face. He also believed a witch was impervious to pain and would use a prodder with a long needle that would retract into the sheath when pressed against the skin so the suspected witch would not feel anything. Another of the "tests" was the swimming test, where a witch would have their thumbs tied to their opposite big toes and be thrown into a river. If they floated they were a witch, yet if they drowned they were innocent.

 Late 1640s—The number of witch trials and executions dropped. This was due in part to the oncoming English Civil War and witches going into hiding.

1682—Temperance Lloyd from Devon became the last witch ever to be executed in England for practicing witchcraft.

 1692–3—The notorious Salem Witch Trials took place in Salem Village, Massachusetts. A group of young girls claimed to have been possessed by the Devil as a result of a number of women performing witchcraft in the area. These claims caused mass hysteria and led to the formation of a special court that tried those accused of witchcraft, leading to 19 hangings. A study published in *Science* magazine in 1976 debunked the myth that some residents had been bewitched with the discovery that a fungus found in food products, such as rye and wheat, which were food staples at the time, caused symptoms such as vomiting, fits, and hallucinations. These symptoms mirrored the ones of those who claimed to have been placed under a witch's spell.

 1735—The Witchcraft Act repealed the acts introduced in the sixteenth and seventeenth centuries and was updated to reflect the modern view that witchcraft and magic were no longer part of the fabric of society but the preserve of the ignorant, superstitious, and criminals. Softer punishments were imposed, such as fines and imprisonment of up to twelve months for anyone who claimed to be able to use magical powers.

1812—*Grimms' Fairy Tales* was published, portraying witches as old women—ones who banished princesses *(Sleeping Beauty)*, lived in gingerbread houses in the woods and ate small children *(Hansel and Gretel)*, and such like. These fairy tales shaped many generations' views of witches and those with magical abilities. There were a few positive witch characters, such as the Fairy Godmother in *Cinderella* and the fairies in *Sleeping Beauty*, who helped to hide a princess from an adversary.

1863—There is evidence of a continuation in vigilante witch hunts, such as a drowning that occurred in Essex, England, of an alleged wizard.

1880s—Pre-Raphaelite artists gave witches an impressive makeover. No longer were they portrayed as repulsive hags but young, beautiful enchantresses, such as in the painting *The Magic Circle* by John William Waterhouse, which shows a beautiful sorceress at her cauldron with a wand in her right hand and a snake looped around her neck. The arresting images created by the Pre-Raphaelite movement proved hugely popular and almost certainly influenced the appearance of the glamorous witches in Disney's *Snow White and the Seven Dwarfs* and *Sleeping Beauty*.

 1951—The last Witchcraft Act was repealed in England, and this was the cue for Gerald Gardner, the founder of modern Wicca, to publish *Witchcraft Today*.

A note

It's important to note that those accused of witchcraft were often Christians who went to church but who also believed in healing powers, the afterlife, and fairies. The church disagreed with these superstitious beliefs, claiming them to be ungodlike and against its teachings. There have also been periods when scholars studied astrology and necromancy, making witchcraft acceptable to the educated few. Also, historical witchcraft is a Christian idea, while contemporary witchcraft is a relatively new concept, forming part of the wider neopaganism movement.

Wizards

Witchcraft is not the sole preserve of women; there are male witches too, although often they prefer to be called wizards. The term "wizard" was widely used in the fifteenth and sixteenth centuries for both male and female practitioners of sorcery, though the name has largely been kept alive in fantasy literature, legends, and folklore. A wizard in a cultural rather than a contemporary context is typically a wise old man with a majestic appearance. He would have a long white beard, a pointed hat, and a voluminous cloak, such as Merlin from Arthurian legend, Gandalf from *The Lord of the Rings*, and, most recently, Albus Dumbledore from the Harry Potter series.

Witches' marks

Ancient symbols have been discovered on buildings across the United Kingdom that were once believed to protect their inhabitants from evil spirits. Many date back from the sixteenth to eighteenth centuries, when houses were poorly lit with tallow candles. Once night fell, it was pitch black. Scratchings and carvings were made near weak entry points, such as doorways and windows—the tangled lines were said to confuse and trap the spirits so they would not enter. Witches' marks have been spotted at Shakespeare's birthplace in Stratford-upon-Avon, the Tower of London, and Wookey Hole in Somerset.

To me, a witch is a woman that is capable of letting her intuition take hold of her actions, that communes with her environment, that isn't afraid of facing challenges.

Paulo Coelho

TOOLS FOR TWENTY-FIRST-CENTURY WITCHCRAFT

We have ascertained that it's not about wearing pointed hats and flying on broomsticks—certainly for the modern witch—but there are a number of items that many witches deem essential to perform spells and rituals. The internet makes light work of finding ingredients and apparatus for spells, and it doesn't have to be a costly exercise. Remember to use what feels right for you—a simple spell can be performed with just a candle and a handful of items gathered from the garden or kitchen cupboard. Here is a list of tools used by witches to practice their spells and rituals.

ALTAR

An altar is a place to focus your thoughts and energies on performing spells and rituals—though it's not always essential for magic. The altar doesn't have to be big—a mantelpiece or small table is adequate. It's the place where you keep all of your tools, such as your wand and book of shadows (see page 44). The four points of the table represent the four elements—earth, air, fire, and water—and items from nature representing these elements should feature on your altar. Think of your altar as being divided into quarters that pertain to the following:

North—represents earth. Items that you can place here to represent earth energies include leaves, twigs, stones, salt, and crystals.

East—represents air. Items to be placed here include feathers, petals, and an oil burner or heatproof dish for burning incense.

South—represents fire. Here place items such as ash, brick, pottery, a small cauldron for burning herbs or paper wishes, and a wand.

 West—represents water. This is the place for collected rainwater in a bowl, seashells, driftwood, and magic stones (stones with a naturally created hole in the middle).

 The center of the altar should contain your candle or candles for spell-casting.

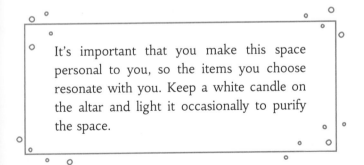

It's important that you make this space personal to you, so the items you choose resonate with you. Keep a white candle on the altar and light it occasionally to purify the space.

Incense—what's best?

Incense is a substance that releases fragrance when burned. It is available in different forms, and it is up to you whether you use oil, cones, powder, or resin chips—one type is not more conducive to spell-casting than another. Oil is popular for witchcraft, as you can use it to anoint candles and heat in an oil burner, but all of the other types can be burned in a heatproof dish or cauldron.

MAGIC WANDS

Wands are often used as a tool for practical magic by the modern-day witch. They are utilized as a way of directing the magic into a particular place and building up energy during a spell. You don't need to spend money on a wand—a twig will do, but you can't just snap it off the nearest tree; you must ask for the blessings of the woods before you take it. Never use green wood, as this is likely to crack. The best wood is that which has fallen from the tree and been left to dry on the ground.

Hazel is traditionally used for wands, as it symbolizes fairness, equality, and wisdom. Other woods you can use include driftwood that has been smoothed by the waves and still contains the energy of the sea.

Wand wood

Think about the types of spells that you wish to perform to help source the most suitable wood. Here are some examples of different woods and their special properties:

Apple—love and family

Ash—clairvoyance and good fortune

Beech—wisdom

Blackthorn—protection

Chestnut—balance

Cypress—for communicating with the dead

Hazel—healing and wisdom

Oak—strength

Rowan—clairvoyance and protection

Willow—healing

Prepare your wand by removing any leaves, then store your wand somewhere indoors to dry out. You can remove the bark and smooth the wood as desired. Some witches carve symbols into the wood or add a crystal to the tip.

Drawing down the moon

Before you can use your wand, you must purify and empower it by the light of a full moon. Stand outside with your wand on a full-moon night and point it at the moon to draw down its power. Other natural phenomena are used to empower a wand; for example, leaving it out in a storm will boost your wand with fearlessness, leaving it in rain will serve to cleanse and purify it, and pointing it toward a rainbow will encourage wish fulfillment.

USING THE WAND

The simplest rituals to perform when using the wand are ones for attraction and repulsion. To attract something, be it luck, love, or good news, circle the tip of the wand in a clockwise motion—start with small circles and gradually increase them as you focus carefully on that which you wish to attract. To maximize your chance of a successful outcome, you must visualize it in as much detail as you can manage. You can use this simple ritual to enchant an object, such as a crystal, or assist with a more complex spell. To detract negativity, circle the tip of the wand in a counterclockwise motion and focus on the thing in your life that you wish to banish.

CANDLES

Candles are a relatively modern addition to spell-casting because it was not until the twentieth century that candles became affordable and easy to come by. The modern witch often casts their spells by candlelight, as the flame provides a focus for their energies and desires. Different colored candles are used depending on the type of spell.

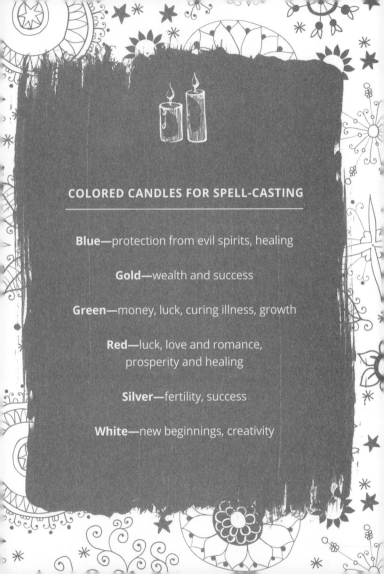

COLORED CANDLES FOR SPELL-CASTING

Blue—protection from evil spirits, healing

Gold—wealth and success

Green—money, luck, curing illness, growth

Red—luck, love and romance,
prosperity and healing

Silver—fertility, success

White—new beginnings, creativity

INCENSE

As with candles, burning incense creates an ambience to help focus your mind when spell-casting. Particular aromas are associated with different beneficial properties depending on the type of spell you are casting:

★ **Acacia**—for clairvoyance

★ **Angelica**—for protection

★ **Basil**—for money and fertility

★ **Bay**—for lifting a curse

★ **Catnip**—for love, happiness, friendship, and courage

★ **Cedar**—to heal a fraught mind

★ **Chamomile**—for a change of luck, circumstance, or prosperity

★ **Cherry**—for love and friendship

★ **Chives**—for banishing negativity

★ **Cinnamon**—to attract money

★ **Clove**—to stop negative words being said about you

★ **Comfrey**—for safe travel and protection

★ **Dill**—to protect new life

★ **Fern**—to encourage rainfall

★ **Frankincense**—for good luck

★ **Garlic**—for protection and dispelling negativity

★ **Lavender**—for good sleep and to attract new love

★ **Mint**—for healing and protection

★ **Patchouli**—for fertility

★ **Pine**—for exorcism and to return negative vibes to their senders

★ **Sage**—to cleanse bad energy and for repulsion spells

★ **Thyme**—for good health and healing

★ **Vetivert**—for protection against thieves and black magic

★ **Willow**—to attract love

★ **Wisteria**—for protection

★ **Ylang-ylang**—adds potency to love and healing spells

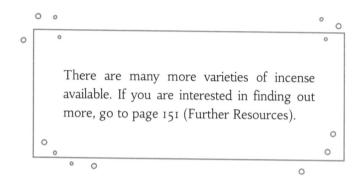

There are many more varieties of incense available. If you are interested in finding out more, go to page 151 (Further Resources).

The power of salt

Salt is a preservative, but not just in the physical sense. It is used in witchcraft for protection and purification. It is believed to draw its magical power from the moon, due to its extraction from water and the moon's pull of the tides. If you are feeling under threat, surround yourself with a line of salt until the feeling has passed. Many witches have salt on their altars for protection when performing spells.

BROOMSTICK

This is a classic symbol of witchcraft, but it isn't generally part of the modern-day witch's arsenal. Sweeping a broom was traditionally a way to clear away malevolent energy in the home and attract the good energy in. For example, if someone unwelcome came to visit, it's believed that they left their negative energy in their footprints, and this was when the broom would have been used to sweep away the bad atmosphere. Leaning a broom across a doorway is believed to ward off enemies and malevolent spirits, and many witches have them in the home as a symbol of their chosen calling.

The classic image of riding a witch's broom is believed to have surfaced from shamanic teachings, when it was used for soul-journeying rituals—the broom would have been held like a hobby horse and the witch would travel metaphorically rather than literally.

BOOK OF SHADOWS

This is essentially a place where a witch records their rituals and spells, much like a diary. It's helpful to keep a reference of when you performed a spell, the ingredients used, the moon's phase, and the outcome. The term was coined by Gerald Gardner, the founder of modern Wicca, as he recommended that the book be kept hidden—"in the shadows"—and private. The traditions of witches and their practices have been kept alive by these books, though many have been lost or destroyed over the years due to the persecution of witches. Many twenty-first-century witches choose to document their practices on a computer—but make sure you back it up!

CAULDRON

Traditionally a large cast-iron vessel with a large mouth and three legs, the cauldron's shape represents Mother Nature and the womb, and the three legs pertain to the three lunar phases: waxing, full, and waning. When placed on or beside an altar, the cauldron represents earth because it has a practical purpose, though it symbolizes all of the elements when in use. Cauldrons are still used today in white witchcraft for mixing herbs, burning incense, and when performing wish spells—powerful hopes are written on paper and burned so that the thoughts enter the ether in curls of smoke.

ATHAME

This is a black-handled, double-edged knife. This is an optional item that is used to inscribe magical words and symbols onto candles.

BELLS

Bells are often used for banishment spells. The bell is rung to settle a bad atmosphere.

CHALICE

This is used as a vessel on the altar to contain water or herbs. It's often used for fertility spells as the bowl of the chalice represents the womb, much like the cauldron.

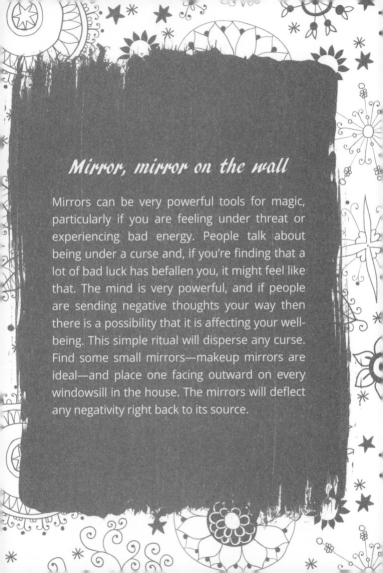

Mirror, mirror on the wall

Mirrors can be very powerful tools for magic, particularly if you are feeling under threat or experiencing bad energy. People talk about being under a curse and, if you're finding that a lot of bad luck has befallen you, it might feel like that. The mind is very powerful, and if people are sending negative thoughts your way then there is a possibility that it is affecting your well-being. This simple ritual will disperse any curse. Find some small mirrors—makeup mirrors are ideal—and place one facing outward on every windowsill in the house. The mirrors will deflect any negativity right back to its source.

The power is within you

There are many other tools that are used in witchcraft, but none are essential because the witch provides the magic with the power of thought and intention. The basic witch's kit consists of candles, a pentacle symbol, a few crystals, and incense.

THE WITCH'S FAMILIAR

A witch's familiar is the witch's animal friend and ally that assists with magical spells. Many animals are associated with witchcraft, but none more so than a black cat. Tales of witches transforming into cats are ubiquitous throughout history—and there are numerous accounts of women being burned as witches due to rumors of them transforming into black cats to cause nightly mischief. These stories give credence to the popular superstition that crossing the path of a black cat will bring bad luck, especially if they happen to be a witch in disguise.

Another animal associated with witchcraft is the bat—in medieval times, a flying bat was believed to be a witch in disguise. In fourteenth-century France, one unfortunate woman was burned at the stake on suspicion of witchcraft because a colony of bats had been seen flying above her home.

Other animals deemed suitable and loyal as familiars are dogs, crows, toads, and ferrets, though elsewhere, baboons are considered the animal most associated with witchcraft and they are still persecuted today because of their association with the magical realm.

Whether you choose to have a black cat (or a baboon!) is up to you.

Witchery
is merely
a word
for what
we are all
capable of.

Charles de Lint

THE POWER OF CRYSTALS

As with all materials forged from nature, gemstones and crystals are alive with magical natural energy. They are used in electrical products due to their conductivity, which makes them the ultimate power source when casting spells. Each stone possesses different energies and properties. Here are some of the most potent:

Agate

This is a soothing and positive stone that will protect the wearer from danger and helps to make sudden changes less daunting.

Amber

If you are experiencing a lot of negativity, wear amber to repel these bad energies. Amber is also the problem solver of crystals, resolving misunderstandings and disagreements.

Amethyst

Place one of these purple crystals by your bed to aid sleep, particularly if you are feeling anxious.

Aquamarine

This ice-blue stone symbolizes hope and good fortune. It's often worn or carried when traveling as it has protective qualities and helps to prevent mishaps.

Carnelian

This fiery orange stone revives and restores. It boosts sensual spells and also helps to cut negative ties that are a drain on your mental and physical well-being.

Fluorite

Fluorescence was first observed in this stone, hence its name. It is a mineral composed of calcium fluoride and is used to absorb negative energy, encouraging positivity and balance. It has healing properties, particularly with ailments relating to skin and the nervous system.

Hematite

The energy in this shiny grey stone aids those with poor circulation and poor concentration, so it's particularly good for long rituals to keep your mind fresh and alert. It's also used in spells to encourage good luck into your life.

Jade

This lush green stone symbolizes longevity and strength. It's used in spells for the attainment of knowledge, specifically information to resolve a difficult situation or conflict.

Lapis lazuli

This deep blue stone pertains to wisdom, intellect, and the healing of headaches and sore throats. It also has clairvoyant properties; lapis jewelry is frequently worn by witches to help them harness their psychic abilities.

Moonstone

This milky white stone has an affinity with its namesake, the moon. It's linked to the lunar phases and with femininity and fertility. It is utilized in spells for clairvoyance and fertility.

Quartz

Clear quartz is one of the most abundant crystals and has the most far-reaching properties of all the crystals. It can be a powerful catalyst in wish spells and aids healing both of physical and emotional imbalances—any situation requiring a positive outcome. If you're beginning on your journey in witchcraft, this crystal makes the ideal companion.

Rose quartz

This pale pink-colored stone is associated with love. Place rose quartz on windowsills to help love flow in and out of your home, and use it for spells to draw love into your life. It's also believed to calm nerves and soothe worries—carry a piece around with you in your pocket when you have a difficult day ahead.

Tiger's eye

With its gold and brown stripes resembling its namesake, it's not surprising that this crystal is utilized for seeing into the future. It's used for spells to help anticipate major events—good and bad—so that you are forewarned. Solutions to upcoming difficulties can also be sought with this stone, and its powers are also called upon in spells to help find employment.

THE POWER OF CRYSTALS

HOW TO LOOK AFTER YOUR CRYSTALS

Keep your crystals safe when they are not being used for spells by placing them in a fabric-lined box or bag. Charge them with energy before a spell by leaving them outside when it's a full moon to soak up the light, or purify them in salt.

Witch stones

Witch stones, also known as hag stones or magic stones, are pebbles or rocks with a naturally occurring hole in the middle. They have many purposes in the realm of witchcraft, including protection at home or when traveling —some fishermen still abide by this and have a string of witch stones hanging on their boats. They are often threaded onto a cord and hung by a window or door, or on a bedstead to ward off nightmares.

Witchcraft...
is a spiritual path.
You walk it for
nourishment
of the soul,
to commune
with the life force
of the universe,
and to thereby
better know your own life.

Christopher Penczak

SIGNS AND SYMBOLS IN WITCHCRAFT

Symbols are very important in white witchcraft. The pentacle is the most recognized of these, but there are many others that have different properties, such as healing, clairvoyance, and fertility. Here are some of the most widely used for spells.

PENTACLE

The pentacle (or pentagram) is a five-point star encased in a circle. It's an important symbol in witchcraft and is considered a potent protection against evil forces. Each point represents an element: earth, air, fire, and water, with the fifth element, the top point, signifying the spirit. The circle around the star represents eternity, the cycle of life and nature, and also acts as a protective field. Some witches wear a pendant depicting a pentacle around their neck as protection and as an unobtrusive way for other witches to notice them.

The pentacle should be present when spells are performed. It's nice to create your own—this could be either drawn on a piece of paper or fashioned from wire or something more elaborate, such as a painting on a plate—the size is irrelevant. Once you have your pentacle symbol, it needs to be exposed to the light of a full moon to charge it with positive and protective energy—it's best to leave your symbol outside overnight. When this is done, the pentacle should remain with you—on your altar or about your person—when you perform your spells.

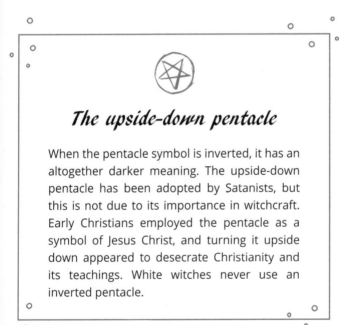

The upside-down pentacle

When the pentacle symbol is inverted, it has an altogether darker meaning. The upside-down pentacle has been adopted by Satanists, but this is not due to its importance in witchcraft. Early Christians employed the pentacle as a symbol of Jesus Christ, and turning it upside down appeared to desecrate Christianity and its teachings. White witches never use an inverted pentacle.

ANKH

This symbol, which looks like a cross with a loop at the top, is the ancient Egyptian symbol for eternal life. It is used in protection spells and to ward off danger.

CELTIC KNOT

This symbol looks like a shield composed of knots and, like the ankh symbol, is seen as a protective talisman. The four corners of the knot represent the elements: earth, air, fire, and water.

EARTH

An upside-down equilateral triangle with a horizontal line inside, which is used in spells to help unify families and encourage good health and prosperity into the home.

AIR

An equilateral triangle with a horizontal line inside, which connects with the soul and our innermost thoughts. It is used in spells for wisdom and improving communication.

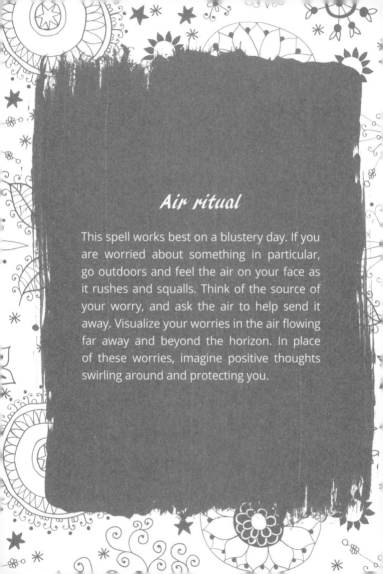

Air ritual

This spell works best on a blustery day. If you are worried about something in particular, go outdoors and feel the air on your face as it rushes and squalls. Think of the source of your worry, and ask the air to help send it away. Visualize your worries in the air flowing far away and beyond the horizon. In place of these worries, imagine positive thoughts swirling around and protecting you.

FIRE

An equilateral triangle symbolizing masculine energy and both destruction and creation. It is used in spells for transformation, growth, and change.

WATER

An upside-down equilateral triangle that symbolizes feminine energy and the moon, which is why this icon is used to cast spells for love and emotions, particularly during a waxing or full moon. It's also used for water scrying (see Fortune-telling Spells, page 121) to aid clairvoyance.

HORNED GOD

A circle with a pair of horns on top is the Wiccan symbol for masculine deities of nature, such as Herne. It is used in fertility rituals.

TRIPLE MOON

This is a full moon with two crescents—one appearing before the full moon, which represents the waxing moon, and the other after the full moon to represent the waning moon. This symbol is also associated with womanhood and is used in empowerment spells and for harnessing the moon's power.

TRIQUETRA

Three interlocking ellipses often used to represent the Holy Trinity in Christianity, but in witchcraft it represents the power of three. Those who have seen the TV series *Charmed* will recognize this symbol, as it is used to represent the combined magical power of the three sisters.

THE WHEEL OF THE YEAR

The circle with eight segments represents the witch's year. Each segment pertains to a Sabbat, which are the seasonal festivals observed by witches and modern pagans: Imbolc, Ostara, Beltane, Litha, Lamas, Mabon, Samhain, and Yule.

Witch runes

These symbols are used for divination and are generally associated with fortune-telling. The symbols are painted on or carved into equal-sized stones, and the person who is having their fortune told must throw the runes like dice. There are eight symbols, ranging from a sun, which can be read as a simple "yes" to your question, to a pair of interlocking rings, which symbolize love and unions. Witches who use runes often carve the symbols into wax for candle spells (see page 142).

MAGICAL DAYS AND TIMES

Timing is important when casting a spell; the day of the week, the phase of the moon, and the time frame in which you choose to perform a spell can have a significant effect on its outcome. For example, a love spell is best performed on a Friday and on a waxing or full moon, and a spell to disperse negativity is more potent during a waning moon phase. This chapter explains why and gives you all the information you need to help you time your spells to their best advantage.

THE PHASES OF THE MOON

The moon has always held a powerful spiritual significance for witches, and many witches cast their spells in accordance with the phases of the moon, as each phase has pertinence to different types of spell. A pocket diary will contain the moon's phases, or you can find this information online.

New moon: NEW BEGINNINGS

This is the perfect time to perform spells that herald new beginnings as the new moon represents positive change. Use the new moon's power for finding employment, new love, or a new home. It's also a potent time for fertility spells.

Waxing moon: GROWTH AND BLOOM

This is when the moon is growing each night until it becomes a full moon. This period is good for attraction spells—ones to grow your wealth, improve health, and draw friends and lovers to your side.

full moon: FULL POWER

This is the most powerful time for magic, so use this period wisely for casting spells for protection, wealth, love, and good health. Some witches experience heightened psychic ability during a full moon.

What if the moon is not visible?

Your spell or ritual will still benefit from the moon's power if it is performed on a cloudy or wet night. Moonlight will obviously enhance the magical atmosphere when spell-casting, but it's not necessary in order to perform spells where the moon's phase is relevant.

Waning moon:
REMOVAL AND LETTING GO

This is when the moon appears to recede each night in the sky. It's the ideal time for repulsion spells, for example, if you want to banish negative forces in your life or want to take control of a difficult situation or soothe a fractious or anxious loved one.

Dark moon: INTROSPECTIVE

This is when the moon appears to be invisible against the backdrop of the sun. This phase occurs three days prior to a new moon. Those who perform dark magic are particularly active at this time, and many white witches choose not to cast spells in this period, while others see it as a good time for spells for breaking negative cycles and bringing justice to bear.

Lunar eclipses

This is another auspicious time to perform spells, especially when you bear in mind that a lunar eclipse only occurs during a full moon, so you are working with full-moon energy. Be particularly careful when performing spells during this time and choose your words and spells wisely.

Can I cast a spell in the daytime?

Spells are traditionally cast in the evening or at night, but a spell can be cast at any time of day, even if it's dependent on a particular moon phase. The time of day really depends on when you can practice in peace and give a spell or ritual your full concentration.

SPELL-CASTING AND
THE DAYS OF THE WEEK

Each day pertains to a planet and a color, and certain spells will have extra resonance when performed on a specific day.

SUNDAY

represented by the sun (unsurprisingly) and the color gold, is the best day for spells pertaining to achieving personal goals, such as finding a job and new revenue streams, and improving self-belief, health, and well-being.

MONDAY

represented by the moon and the color silver, is ideal for spells related to family and healing.

TUESDAY

represented by Mars and the color red, is for spells of passion, though not necessarily affairs of the heart—it could be a personal goal that you wish to achieve.

WEDNESDAY

represented by Mercury and the color yellow, is a particularly good day for casting money and business spells.

THURSDAY

represented by Jupiter and the color blue, brings strength to spells associated with partnerships—these could be personal as well as professional. All aspects of learning and gaining wisdom are also strong themes on this day.

FRIDAY

represented by Venus and the color pink, is for love spells, as well as ones for fertility and creativity.

SATURDAY

represented by Earth and the color brown, is for spells that signify endings as well as fresh starts, and for banishing bad habits.

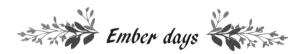

Ember days

These magical days appear four times a year, before a solstice or equinox, and are regarded as "threshold" times when witches are more powerful yet vulnerable to malicious spirits. These days are used for performing protection spells against negative forces in preparation for the birth of the new season.

Halloween

Halloween is an important date for pagans, as it coincides with their new year, also known as Samhain, which is one of the four most sacred days in the Wiccan calendar. It's the ideal date for performing spells to help reach personal and professional goals in the coming year.

The other sacred days for Wiccans, which are linked to the cycles of the moon, are Imbolc (February 1), Beltane (April 30) and Lammas (July 31).

PRACTICAL MAGIC

How do spells work?

The mind is the witch's most powerful tool. Witchcraft aside, when you focus on your intentions and goals, and map these out either by writing a list or visualizing them as pictures on a mood board, it achieves positive results. In the same way, casting a spell employs the power of positive thinking, like meditative visualization. These thoughts are combined with the magical energies in nature by employing the four elements—earth, air, fire, and water—via naturally occurring materials, such as crystals and incense, which become the focus of your energies for the spell.

There are no restrictions as to what items you use to perform a spell, as long as it has a resonance and personal connection for you in relation to the spell that you are casting. The spells outlined in the following chapters are a guide, and it's encouraged that you work instinctively to make the spell personal to you to maximize its power.

Chakras and spells

Many white witches believe their inner power comes from their chakras, which are energy points in the body. The word "chakra" is Sanskrit for wheel or disc, and chakra cleansing is part of some yoga disciplines, such as Ayurveda, and holistic therapies, such as reiki. There are seven chakras in the body and each is associated with a particular characteristic and color, as follows:

CROWN

at the top of the head. It is associated with spirituality and inner and outer beauty.

Color: violet

BROW

also known as the "third eye chakra," located in the middle of the forehead. It relates to psychic abilities and intuition.

Color: indigo

THROAT

located at the throat. This is related to self-expression, communication, and creativity.

Color: blue

HEART

at the heart. This chakra is linked with feelings of love, both of others and oneself.

Color: green

SOLAR PLEXUS

at the naval. It relates to inner power and strength.

Color: yellow

SACRAL

located near the prostate for men or ovaries for women. It pertains to sexual health and emotional balance.

Color: orange

ROOT

located at the base of the spine in the tailbone. It relates to being grounded and balanced.

Color: red

You will notice that the colors are that of a rainbow. This is significant when choosing crystals for spell-casting, as the color will give you a clear indication as to its properties in relation to the human mind and body. For example, green is associated with the heart chakra, so green-colored stones, like jade and emerald, are used to balance emotions; blue stones, such as lapis lazuli, aid communication and clear speech, whereas violet amethyst will help attune to your powers of foresight and increase spiritual awareness.

A simple way to connect with your chakras and your inner power is through meditation. Light seven candles—one of each color that represents a chakra point. Then, beginning with the root chakra, focus on one chakra at a time from root to crown. If you are experiencing an imbalance in a particular area, try a meditation with just one colored candle that corresponds to that chakra. An alternative meditation is to use a corresponding crystal, placing it on the chakra, and take calming breaths, while imagining healing energy flowing through your body. For more information on chakras and holistic healing, see Further Resources (page 151).

PREPARING TO PERFORM MAGIC

In order to be in the right mindset for casting a spell, you must clear your head of outside influences, thoughts, and worries. One of the best ways to quiet the mind is to perform a mindfulness exercise. There are many different forms of meditation that you can explore, but this simple exercise will get you started.

Sit somewhere quiet, where you won't be disturbed for ten minutes or so. Light a candle and focus on the flame. Allow your eyes to glaze as you watch the flame dance. Listen to the sounds around you and notice what thoughts are in your mind. Tune in to your body. Focus on your breathing and allow your stomach to rise and fall. Imagine that you are breathing in the candlelight. Visualize each breath flooding your body with golden light from the candle. Once you feel calm, focused, and energized, you are ready to perform your spell.

THINGS TO CONSIDER BEFORE SPELL-CASTING

 Make sure your intentions are good—this is especially so when you are casting a love spell or a spell that will affect another person. If you are prone to crushes, for example, and you want your crush to take notice of you, be prepared for the attention, as you might change your mind and a spell of this nature is hard to undo.

 Consider the phase of the moon, as it's important to perform the spell at the right time. For example, you don't want to be casting a money spell on a waning moon as it might have the opposite effect. See page 70 for information on moon phases.

 Believe in yourself! As with trying anything new in life, you're bound to be a little hesitant when you start to perform spells and are likely to doubt your abilities. Believe that you can do it, and you will!

Loud and clear

Words can play a powerful role when casting a spell, so make your voice as well as your intentions clear. Often, saying the words out loud, rather than whispering or transmitting them as thoughts, helps the spell to manifest that bit quicker, but make sure you're out of everyone's earshot at the time. It works in a similar way to speaking affirmations out loud—try this exercise and see how much better you feel:

1   Take advantage of a quiet moment in the day and sit somewhere with a nice view—it could be the view from a window in your home, or perhaps you have a picture that you find particularly uplifting.

2   Say the words *I'm grateful for all the good things I have in my life* as you look at the view or picture.

3   Listen to your voice as you speak these words and repeat them several times.

4   It should leave you feeling positive and with a sense of trust in the order of life.

PREPARING YOUR ALTAR

The altar is your special place for casting spells and should be cleansed before performing a spell or ritual. This can be done by simply lighting a white candle and imagining white protective light encircling your altar. You can also use a wand by drawing a clockwise circle in the air above your altar, again imagining a protective light around it.

SPELLS AND RITUALS

Now that you have created an altar to work at and have the basic tools necessary for witchcraft, you can begin casting spells. Here are some spells and rituals to try:

When you look
at a field of
dandelions,
you can either see
a hundred weeds
or a thousand wishes.

Anonymous

LOVE SPELLS

A SPELL TO MAKE
A PARTICULAR PERSON THINK OF YOU

Moon phase: waxing or full
Day of the week: Friday evening

You will need:

A red, white, or pink candle
A photograph of the person or their name
written on a piece of paper
Cherry incense
A cauldron or heatproof dish

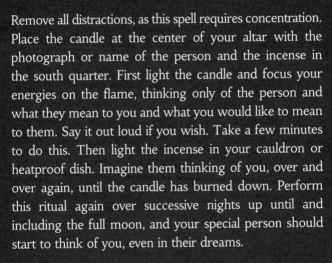

Remove all distractions, as this spell requires concentration. Place the candle at the center of your altar with the photograph or name of the person and the incense in the south quarter. First light the candle and focus your energies on the flame, thinking only of the person and what they mean to you and what you would like to mean to them. Say it out loud if you wish. Take a few minutes to do this. Then light the incense in your cauldron or heatproof dish. Imagine them thinking of you, over and over again, until the candle has burned down. Perform this ritual again over successive nights up until and including the full moon, and your special person should start to think of you, even in their dreams.

Case study: a spell to attract a lover

I heard of this spell from a witch friend. She was interested in someone from her neighborhood and, though she tried to get him to notice her over a long period of time, all her efforts had proved fruitless. She first made sure that he was single and then decided to seek advice from a fellow witch, who suggested the following ritual. They prepared a meal one evening with candles to focus their energies. Then she voiced her intentions out loud, after which she placed a ball of rice in her mouth and had to eat the whole thing without taking bites out of it* as a kind of ritual to prove that she was serious of her intentions. They ended the ritual with the following words:

[Name] notice me,
Seek my love
So mote it be!

They allowed the candle to burn down and extinguish itself. The very next day, the man came up to her in the cafe where she was working and asked her out on a date. She almost collapsed with shock, but it seems their love was meant to be as they've been married for ten years.

*Be careful if you try to emulate this spell that you don't choke on too much food—exercise common sense and only use a small amount!

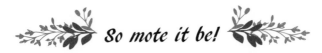

So mote it be!

This may seem a mysterious phrase to say at the end of a spell, but it is common in neopagan rituals and modern-day witchcraft. It means "so may it be" or "so it is required" and affirms the intent of the spell, similar to saying "amen" at the end of a prayer.

A SPELL TO DETRACT A RIVAL

- -

It can be very unsettling when someone is making a play for your beloved. This spell will kindly but firmly see them on their way.

Moon phase: waning
Day of the week: any

You will need:

A small card and envelope (gift-tag size)
Sealing wax
A plastic box with a lid
Water

Write the name of the person that is pursuing your partner on the card and place it in the envelope. Seal the envelope with the wax, then put it in the plastic container, fill the container with water, and place the lid on. Say the following words out loud: *Take your love away from my love. So mote it be.* Pop the plastic container in the freezer and their charms should settle on someone new.

A SPELL TO MAKE YOU IRRESISTIBLE ON A DATE

Moon phase: full

Day of the week: Tuesday, Thursday, or Friday

You will need:

A red or pink candle

A magnet, small enough to fit in the bag

A pocket-sized bag

Your favorite perfume (or cologne)

Place the candle, the magnet, the bag, and the perfume bottle onto your altar before you go out on your date. Light the candle and spray a small amount of your perfume over the altar. Say the following words: *Tonight I will shine. I am irresistible. This night is mine. So mote it be.*

Repeat the words as you spray on your perfume (not too much!) then place the magnet in the bag. Allow the candle to burn as you get ready, then blow it out and place the bag containing the magnet in your pocket or purse before you go out for the evening.

Love ritual

For a simple ritual to give your love life a boost, place two pieces of rose quartz, a photo of you and your partner, and two pink candles on your altar. Light the candles and think about your partner and what you love about them. Allow the candles to burn down and place the rose quartz stones under your bed. Practice this spell on a new, waxing, or full moon on any given day.

A word of warning

There's nothing more tantalizing than to attract new love with a spell, but tread carefully and be clear and honest as to your intentions. Don't set out to bewitch someone away from their partner and don't try to win back your ex without reminding yourself why you broke up with them in the first place, or you may regret the results! Don't be impatient if you are attracted to someone—allow things to happen naturally and get to know them a little first before casting a spell to make you more attractive to them. After all, you don't want someone pining for you after you've decided they're not the one.

HAPPINESS AND
GOOD-FORTUNE SPELLS

WISHING BUBBLES

Moon phase: new
Day of the week: any

You will need:

Incense
A cauldron or heatproof dish
Bubble mixture and wand

Begin by burning the incense in your cauldron or heat-proof dish. Allow the scent to permeate the air, and pass the bottle of bubbles over it a few times. While doing so, concentrate on your wish and the ideal outcome—imagine it in as much detail as you can. Then take your mixture outside to a quiet spot and blow your bubbles. With each breath, imagine you are filling the bubbles with your wish. Watch the bubbles fly off into the sky, full of your intentions—as they pop the wish is released.

MONEY-GROWING SPELL

Moon phase: new, waxing, or full
Day of the week: Thursday, Saturday, or Sunday

You will need:

A pinch of dried patchouli leaves
A healthy basil plant
A coin of any denomination

Sprinkle the patchouli over the soil around the base of your basil plant. Take your coin and place it vertically in the soil so that it resembles a half moon. When money comes to you, spend the coin and replace it with another so the luck continues. Don't forget to keep tending the plant so it thrives.

A MONEY SPELL FOR DIFFICULT TIMES

Moon phase: new
Day of the week: Wednesday, Thursday, or Saturday

You will need:

A pencil
A piece of paper
A small green dish
A green candle

Write down the amount of money you need, and supply a legitimate reason as to why you need it—don't be greedy. Fold the piece of paper in half and place it under the dish. Put the candle on the dish and light it. Concentrate on the burning candle and imagine receiving the money. Once the candle has burned down (extinguishing itself) and cooled, wrap the remaining small disc of wax in the piece of paper and carry it in your purse or wallet.

A SIMPLE RITUAL FOR GOOD LUCK

Moon phase: new, waxing, or full
Day of the week: any

Assemble a small group of like-minded friends or relatives and stand in a small circle. In the middle of the circle, place a bowl of ripe apples. Each person must pick an apple. Then, when everyone has an apple to hold, each person in turn must make a wish (it can be silent or out loud, though articulating a wish out loud often helps in the same way as when making affirmations). Once everyone in the group has made a wish, you must eat the apples together to complete the spell.

EMPLOYMENT AND SUCCESS-AT-WORK SPELLS

A SPELL FOR EMPLOYMENT

This spell is best performed at the beginning of your job search.

Moon phase: begin on the
new moon and end on the full moon

Day of the week: begin on a
Wednesday, Thursday, or Sunday

You will need:

A brown candle
A candle of the color of your choice
A green candle
Bergamot oil

Place the three candles on your altar and dab some bergamot oil on each of the wicks—this oil represents good fortune in work endeavours. First, light the candle that you have picked with a color that resonates with you. As you do so, visualize the type of job that you would like to have. Try to imagine the kind of tasks you would be undertaking and think about how fulfilled you will feel. Say the following words: *I wish for a job. It is my right. Clear the way and bring my goal in sight.* Next, light the green candle, which represents money, and say the following words: *Bring luck and abundance, let prosperity flow to me.* Imagine receiving payment for your work. Finally, light the brown candle, which represents your future job, and say the words: *Bring this work opportunity to me. So mote it be.* Repeat this spell once a day until the full moon or until you have your new job.

A SPELL TO HELP YOU FOCUS

If you're prone to daydreaming in meetings or browsing Twitter when you should be finishing a report, then this spell will help you to gain focus and reach your career goals. Rosemary was worn by ancient Greek scholars, as they believed it made them wiser.

Moon phase: new
Day of the week: any

You will need:

Water
Mug
A few sprigs of freshly picked rosemary—pick it on a new moon and when the plant is not flowering
A teaspoon of sugar or honey
Rosemary oil
Hand cream

Boil some water and pour it into a mug, then add your sprigs of rosemary and let it infuse for a few minutes. Add a teaspoon of sugar or honey to sweeten it, remove the rosemary sprig, and then drink the infusion before heading off to work. Make up some rosemary-scented hand cream by adding a few drops of the oil to your cream and mixing it. Just before a meeting or a work situation when you need to be at your most alert and intelligent, rub some of this cream on your hands and your temples to stimulate your mind.

BONUS SPELL

This is ideal for when you are vying for a pay raise or bonus, or any form of sudden increase in wealth, whether it is "due" to you or not. If money isn't due to you and you would just like more of it, consider a figure and the purpose for which you will use it. Above all, don't be greedy, and always share your good fortune, even if it's just a donation to the charity box.

Moon phase: waxing to full moon
Day of the week: Wednesday or Sunday

You will need:

Peony incense
A cauldron or heatproof dish
A white candle
A yellow candle
An athame—or, if you don't have one, a
pin or sharp pen nib will do the job
A length of gold ribbon

Begin by burning some of the incense in your cauldron. Light a white candle on your altar, then take the yellow candle and heat one side of it over the flame to soften the wax for carving. Be careful when you do this—it won't take long. Once the wax is soft enough, take your athame or pin and carve your name in cursive writing on the side of the candle. Then place the yellow candle on your altar and light it. Watch the flame and imagine how you will feel when money arrives, then specify a date by which you would like to receive the money and thank the candle. Light the candle over consecutive days up until the full moon, and all the while focus on your goals. Once the candle has burned down to a tiny nub, extinguish the flame and wait for it to cool. Then tie the gold ribbon around it and carry it around with you until the spell has been granted.

A lucky charm for employment

Keep a tiger's eye stone in your pocket, as this will help to draw good luck when searching for a job. If you have been offered an interview, keep the stone with you in your bag or pocket for luck.

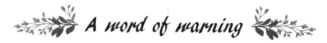

A word of warning

If you are casting a spell to find a job, the spell won't be doing your job search for you—you still need to be proactive and apply for positions and network. These spells will bring energy to your desires, but it's up to you to take advantage of the opportunities that come your way. If you apply for a job and you're not successful, view this setback as a sign that the universe has other, better plans for you.

PROTECTION AND
GOOD-HEALTH SPELLS

FIRE SPELL TO DISPEL
BAD HABITS OR OBSESSIONS

If you're struggling to kick a habit, be it smoking or gossiping or something else, this cauldron spell will help.

Moon phase: waning
Day of the week: Monday, Saturday, or Sunday

You will need:

A red candle
A cauldron or heatproof dish
A black candle
A sprinkling of chile, ginger, and sage
A very small piece of charcoal
Something that symbolizes your bad habit, such as a wine label or an empty packet of cigarettes

Place your red candle to the left of your cauldron or heatproof dish and light it, saying the words: *Red is for strength and power. Help me to kick this bad habit, every day and every hour.* Then place the black candle to the right of your cauldron, light it, and say: *Black has the power to send things away. Give me the power to finish this today.* Place the herbs in the heatproof dish with the charcoal. Rip up the item that symbolizes your bad habit and place in the dish. Light the contents of the dish and say: *Burn away and end your control over me. I will be free. So mote it be.* Allow the contents of the dish to burn and imagine yourself rejecting your habit. Allow the candles to burn down so that they extinguish themselves.

Warning: Be very careful when using a cauldron or heatproof dish, as they get incredibly hot when lit—make sure it is on a secure, heatproof surface and do not leave your lit cauldron unattended!

A PROTECTION SPELL

If you are feeling anxious about the day ahead—perhaps you have a meeting with someone whom you don't see eye to eye with or you're going somewhere new—this ritual with a wand will ease your nerves.

Moon phase: any
Day of the week: any

You will need:

A wand

Take your wand in the hand you use to write with and make a circle in front of you at arm's length in a clockwise motion. Do this nine times, as nine represents intellectual power and influence over situations. This spell will create a circle of protection around you for the day. This ritual can be performed on any given day.

HEALING RITUAL

Moon phase: waning
Day of the week: Sunday

This is a lovely spell for healing a broken heart or an unquiet mind. Take a solo trip to a pebble beach—this can be any time of day but is probably safest in the daytime due to the tides and access. Take off your socks and shoes and walk in the waves. Feel the energy of the water as it laps against your ankles. While walking, look for a pebble in the water that will fit comfortably in your palm. Pick up the pebble and focus all of your negativity and hurt into the pebble. Once you have shed all negative thoughts, cast the pebble back into the sea so that the natural force of the water releases and heals your sorrow.

A SPELL FOR SOMEONE IN NEED

This is for when someone you care about is unwell or facing tough times in their personal life.

Moon phase: new or waxing
Day of the week: Monday or Sunday

You will need:

A length of green ribbon (long enough to tie a bow)
A rose quartz crystal
A photo of the person in need (if you have one)
A green candle
A potted basil plant

Wrap the ribbon around the crystal and hold it tightly in your writing hand. Place the photo beside the candle on your altar and then light the candle. Imagine protective yellow light encircling the person in need until the candle has burned down. Then give the rose quartz wrapped in the ribbon and the basil plant to your friend. Keep sending love and light to them and they will feel supported and hopeful.

A CLEANSING SPELL

- -

Moon phase: new
Day of the week: any
Time of day: evening, before bed

You will need:

A small red drawstring bag
Oak leaves
An acorn
Half a lemon

If you feel you have been tarred with bad luck for too long, this spell will cleanse away any ill will and leave good fortune in its place. Collect a bag full of oak leaves—preferably ones that have been shed—and a single acorn. Take them home and wash them in water to remove any dirt. Fill a bath with warm water and scatter the leaves in it. Then squeeze the lemon half over the water. Hold the acorn in your hand and imagine positivity and happiness entering your life. Climb into the bath and enjoy the oak leaves on your skin and the smell of the lemon, making you feel cleansed and protected. When you have finished your bath, place the acorn under your pillow to encourage restful sleep and positive dreams. Wake early, preferably before sunrise. Take your acorn outside and expose it to the sun, all the while thinking positive thoughts, then place the acorn in your red drawstring bag and carry it with you in your pocket or handbag. The acorn is now infused with luck and positivity. At every new moon, make a wish on your acorn for good fortune and lasting happiness.

Case study: unifying spell

If you are having problems with a particular person—it could be a family member, friend, or acquaintance—this spell can help to smooth the waters. It's important to add some thought into the items you use to perform your spell. Some people use crystals and will pick one or two that resonate with them, while others will use natural elements, such as leaves or stones—take your time to consider the elements you will use before you cast your spell.

One example of this spell was an attempt to unify two former friends who didn't see eye to eye, which had led to some unpleasant exchanges. The friend on the receiving end of these exchanges picked two precious stones from a selection—one was amethyst, which is used for calm and balance, and the other was rose quartz, which is used for strengthening relationships and support. A raw egg was cracked and the contents discarded—the egg in this instance represented friendship and rebirth. The crystals were placed in the shell and the egg was put back together and then buried in the earth outdoors. The spell had the desired result and the angry friend calmed down and became much more amenable.

FORTUNE-
TELLING SPELLS

WATER SPELL FOR CLAIRVOYANCE

Moon phase: new
Day of the week: any

You will need:

A cauldron or heatproof dish
A candle
Mugwort—preferably dried (you can purchase it online)
Water

Fill your cauldron with water. Light your candle and remove other light sources. Sprinkle the mugwort over the water and wait for it to settle. Focus on the surface of the water and think of a burning question that you have, then wait for images to appear to guide you toward an answer. The mugwort will create shapes, but witches claim to see images too. This spell takes practice, but it's a great way to use your cauldron.

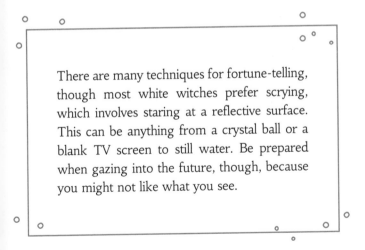

There are many techniques for fortune-telling, though most white witches prefer scrying, which involves staring at a reflective surface. This can be anything from a crystal ball or a blank TV screen to still water. Be prepared when gazing into the future, though, because you might not like what you see.

Prediction candle spell

Here's a simple spell if you want a question answered. It requires a beeswax candle and a dark room, so it's best to do this at night at your altar. Light the candle and allow it to burn for a few minutes. Then ask a question and keep a watchful eye on the flame—restrict the questions to ones that only require a "yes" or "no" answer.

If the flame starts to bounce and jump, then the answer is "yes." If the flame dips or goes out, then the answer is "no," and if sparks fly, then the outcome will be determined by a force beyond your power.

Once finished with your questions, extinguish the flame. Keep this candle purely for prediction spells.

NEW BEGINNINGS AND FRESH-START SPELLS

NEW RESOLUTIONS SPELL

Moon phase: waning

Day of the week: Saturday—at any time of the day

You will need:

A large basket or dish
Autumn leaves

This spell is best performed in the autumn, as it requires a copious quantity of dried leaves. It's a nice one to do with a small group of friends or close family members and could become an annual ritual to celebrate autumn and the year to come. Collect a basket or large dish full of fallen leaves—they can be from any tree—and place it in the center of your dining or coffee table. Assemble everyone around the table, then ask each person in turn to pick up a leaf and say out loud what they want to discard for the next year, before discarding the leaf on the ground. It could be a negative relationship, a bad habit, a health complaint, etc. Keep going around the table until the leaves are gone. Once finished, sweep up the leaves and compost them! Think of the things that you are letting go of breaking down into the earth, as the leaves decompose, and new positive things growing and flourishing in their place.

A SPELL TO RE-ESTABLISH CONTACT WITH SOMEONE FROM YOUR PAST

- -

With Facebook, Twitter, and LinkedIn, it's much easier to stay in touch with friends both old and new, but if you can't find the digital breadcrumbs that lead to a particular person, then this spell is for you.

Moon phase: new

Day of the week: Monday, Wednesday, or Thursday

You will need:

Sandalwood incense

A photograph of your friend and a personal item that connects the two of you

A white candle

A cauldron or heatproof dish

Sea salt

A shallow dish containing water

Begin by lighting the incense on your altar, and allow the smoke to spread and the smell to permeate the air. Place the photograph of your friend on your altar with your personal item—this could be something that they have given you or that conjures up memories of happy times you have spent together. Light the candle in the cauldron or heatproof dish and think about your friend. Take a handful of sea salt and sprinkle it into the dish; while doing so say the following words: *Contact me, so mote it be*. Repeat the words several times, then focus again on your shared memories while the candle burns down. Your friend should get in touch before the salted water has evaporated.

EMPOWERMENT RITUAL

Moon phase: waxing and full
Day of the week: any

This ritual is for adding fuel to a dream or desire. It's a noisy ritual and must be done outdoors as it involves setting off fireworks. Consider your dream when choosing the color of your fireworks: If your dream revolves around wealth, then pick golds and greens; if the spell is for love, choose red and pink; for healing and purification, choose white. The fireworks need to be left on your altar or an image of a pentacle for the days leading up to the full moon. On the night of the full moon, set up the fireworks in a safe, open place in your yard and as you do so, concentrate on your goal and visualize the outcome. Then light the fireworks—being careful to adhere to the safety instructions—and as they burst, light up the sky, and rain down in their colors, the wish is released.

TWENTY-FIRST-CENTURY
SPELL-CASTING

It's fun to use the same apparatus for spell-casting that has been used for centuries, but some spells can be performed with the most modern gadgetry. Think of the amount of energy required when rebooting a computer or sending a text—this surge of power can be harnessed by the twenty-first-century witch for successful spell-casting.

TEXT SPELLS

Text spells require a willing participant, as you will need to send your text spell to someone and for them to send it back to you. As with all other types of spells, the intention must be clear, and for an extra boost, use the moon phases to help you. Think of something specific that you would like to happen, for example, "I want to get an interview for the [insert job title] job." Send this as a text to your like-minded friend; ask them to send a text back to you with the same message, but ask them to reword the text so it includes your name instead of "I" and end the text with "So mote it be." If the spell hasn't worked within the week, try it again, as sometimes spells can't be forced into a time frame and they'll happen when they're ready. Don't delete the texts until the spell has been successful.

EMAIL SPELLS

These are very similar to text spells. Think of an intention and be as clear and succinct as possible, preferably restricting your spell to one sentence, and then write "So mote it be" underneath. Write the type of spell in the subject line and send it to your friend— perhaps tell them beforehand that you are going to do this. Ask them to open the spell and then send it back to you. Do this once a day for a week—so that you alternately send the email every day. Your spell should work within one month.

A SPELL FOR SOMEONE IN PARTICULAR TO MAKE CONTACT WITH YOU

If you're waiting for someone to call, it can be maddening to keep looking at your phone or emails, only to find there is nothing there. This spell will help to speed up the response, whether you're awaiting the outcome of a job interview or for a date to get in touch.

Moon phase: new, waxing, or full
Day of the week: any

You will need:

A pen
A sticky note
Your cell phone or tablet—whichever device you
regularly use to send and receive messages
A sprinkle of each of the following dried herbs:
dill, caraway, and oregano

Write down the name of the person you want to contact you (or the company name if you don't have a specific contact name) on the sticky note. Place the sticky note on your phone or tablet and put it on your altar, then scatter the herbs in a clockwise motion around your device. Visualize the person either picking up the phone to call you or sending you an email, and imagine the words you want them to say or write—be as specific as you can. Then say the following words: *Herbs and magic Mercury, speed to me the call/text/email I wish to receive. So mote it be!*

Leave your device for a few hours, or overnight if you are performing the spell in the evening. Try not to think about it anymore and go about your day, and you will hear from them very soon.

WISH SPELLS WHILE REBOOTING OR MAKING TEA

Consider the amount of power required each time to reboot a computer, turn on the monitor, or even make coffee. This energy can be used for quick wish spells. You will need a sticky note and a pen. Write a wish that you would like to come true. Don't be greedy and ask for a million dollars, because you won't get it—ask for a specific amount for something that you need, or, if you want to make a wish for someone else, add their name to the wish. Write "So mote it be" underneath your spell. Then switch on the computer until it's running or the coffeemaker until it's ready and focus your mind on the spell, visualizing the outcome as clearly as possible.

Why hasn't my spell worked?

It can be easy to become skeptical about the power of witchcraft when a spell doesn't go as planned, but there are good reasons why some spells simply won't work or produce a surprisingly different result to the one you hoped for. Here are some reasons why a spell might not be effective:

★ You might not have been in the right frame of mind to focus fully on the spell. Your mind is the most powerful aspect of spell-casting, so if your mind is elsewhere, then the magic will not happen.

★ If you're unwell or upset, you're not going to be able to give your full attention to a spell—allow yourself to rest and recuperate first.

★ If you have cast a spell to win the lottery, then you're highly likely to be disappointed. The reason for this is that when you conjure money, you will only get what you need and nothing more. When you do receive money, as a result of a spell, be sure to give a small amount away so that you share your good luck.

★ A love spell to force someone to fall in love with you is equally unlikely to work, because it is wrong to try to influence a person's thoughts and feelings.

No matter how important everything else is to magical success, belief is the most crucial.

Dorothy Morrison

HOW TO DEVISE
YOUR OWN SPELLS

This chapter explains how to tailor your own spells. The most straightforward spells that can be adapted for your own purposes are candle spells and wish bag spells. Once you have tried existing spells, it can be fun to create your own. It's straightforward to do, and the more you apply your own instincts and thoughts to a spell, the greater likelihood of success. Here's a simple guide to get you started.

First you need to think about the premise of the spell and the goal that you are aiming for. It could be to get someone to notice you, to receive good news about a job application, or even for a bit of good luck to enter your life.

- -

Think about the components required to perform the spell. Symbolism is very important when it comes to spell-casting. A candle is a good way of focusing your thoughts, as are items that are pertinent to you and the motivation behind your spell—anything that has a special meaning to you, such as a handwritten note or a piece of jewelry.

- -

Consider the timing before you perform your spell—pay attention to the phases of the moon and the day of the week. See the Magical Days and Times chapter (page 69) for further information.

Decide if you want to use the power of thought or would rather say a few words to affirm your spell. This could be a simple sentence to clarify the aim of the spell, which you repeat over and over again, or, if you're particularly good with words, you could write a rhyming couplet. Think carefully about the words before you say them—write them down as a prompt.

Once you have all of the above elements in place, you are ready to perform your spell. Make sure that you record and date your spell in your book of shadows, along with the end result.

CANDLE SPELLS

There are three processes to complete prior to performing a candle spell: charging, carving, and dressing.

CHARGING

This is when you transmit your hopes, wishes, and desires to the candle by holding it, closing your eyes, and focusing fully on your goals. Take your time with this—those who practice meditation are particularly good at charging candles.

CARVING

This is when you carve words, symbols, or images into the wax to personalize the candle. For example, if you wanted to create a candle for someone in need of luck, you would add lucky symbols, such as a star and their name, and perhaps a good luck message pertaining to achieving a specific goal. The more intricate and personal the candle, the greater the likelihood the spell will work.

DRESSING

This is when you add embellishments to the candle, such as drops of essential oil, dried flowers, or glitter.

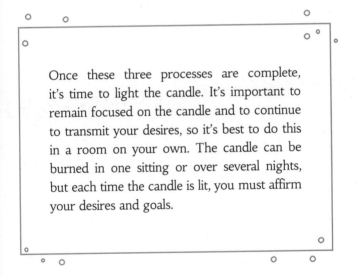

Once these three processes are complete, it's time to light the candle. It's important to remain focused on the candle and to continue to transmit your desires, so it's best to do this in a room on your own. The candle can be burned in one sitting or over several nights, but each time the candle is lit, you must affirm your desires and goals.

WISH BAGS

As with candle magic, this is a creative form of spell-casting and one of the nicest ways of performing a spell for another person. It takes time, but the results—as long as the intentions are good—are worth it. Wish bags traditionally contain one or more objects that can then be carried discreetly in a pocket or purse. Ingredients that can be used include crystals or semiprecious stones (see list of stones and their magical properties on page 52) and small items significant to a spell, such as a small carved object, earth, seeds, or pips—the options are infinite. The intention of the wish bag should be written clearly on a sheet of white paper. Like the candle spell, the items can be "dressed" with oils or glitter. The wish bags are often made from red felt, but any fabric can be used, and it's up to you how elaborate you make it. As with candles, different colors (of fabric and stones) pertain to different spells (see page 39).

To charge your wish bag with magical energy, place it next to a candle that has been carved and dressed. Light the candle and focus your energy on visualizing the outcome of the spell, or imagine the obstacles falling away in order for you to reach your goal. These spells can be performed over several days until the candle has burned down, then you can carry your wish bag around with you until the spell has worked. Alternatively, if the wish bag is for a friend in need, give them the wish bag and carved candle. Instruct them to light the candle when they have a quiet moment and focus on their wish while holding the bag. The candle can be lit over several days until it has burned down. Encourage your friend to keep the wish bag with them, either on their desk or bedside table or in a pocket or purse.

Ideas for charms to place in your spell bag:

 Acorn: luck, prosperity, and sexual potency

 Clover: life, luck, and abundance

 Horn: repels the "evil eye" and is a symbol of nature, fertility, and sexuality

 Horseshoe: luck

 Key: power and luck, especially if it is found and the finder does not know which lock it opens. A symbol of access to hidden things

Lightning-struck wood: protection against all harm

 Pine cone: luck, favorable influences, protection from harm, and repels bad influences

 Religious symbol: symbols of various religions are held to be protective

 Salt: purification, repels evil

 Silver: protection and wealth

WITCH'S LADDER

Not all spells require an armory of tools and magic-infused objects. A humble piece of string can be utilized for some powerful wish magic to create a witch's ladder. A foot-long strand will suit this type of spell-casting.

Nine days before the full moon, begin your witch's ladder by tying a knot in the string—be careful to tie the knot toward you as you visualize the fruition of your wish. Each night, tie a new knot until the night of the full moon. Leave your witch's ladder outside to be charged by the full moon. The knots will hold the power for your wish to be realized. To help you to visualize the outcome of your spell, use these words when tying each knot:

With knot one, the spell has begun.
With knot two, the magic is true.
With knot three, so mote it be.
With knot four, the spell's power is stored.
With knot five, the spell's power will thrive.
With knot six, the spell is fixed.
With knot seven, the future I leaven.
With knot eight, my spell is my fate.
With knot nine, what's done is mine.
So mote it be!

Hang up your ladder in a place where you will see it on a regular basis, such as by your desk or in your bedroom. Once the ladder has served its purpose, bury it in the yard to release the energy back into the earth.

You can add objects to the knots to boost the spell, such as a few strands of your hair or someone else's if the spell is for another person, crystal beads that pertain to the energy that you wish to attract (see The Power of Crystals, page 51), charms (see page 146), or herbs (see page 40).

People only see
what they are
prepared to see.

Ralph Waldo Emerson

FURTHER RESOURCES

The information in this beginner's guide to white witchcraft is essentially the tip of the iceberg and is designed to help you determine the areas in which you would like to study further. Here are some of my favorite books and websites:

BOOKS

Cornish, Sophie. *Witchcraft: A Beginner's Guide to Witchcraft* (CreateSpace Independent Publishing Platform, 2015)

Grant, Ember. *The Book of Crystal Spells* (Llewellyn Productions, 2013)

Greenaway, Leanna and Robbins, Shawn. *Wiccapedia: A Modern-Day White Witch's Guide* (Sterling, 2014)

Hardie, Titania. *Titania's Book of Hours: A Celebration of the Witch's Year* (Quadrille Publishing Ltd., 2002)

Illes, Judika *The Element Encyclopedia of 5000 Spells* (Element, 2004)

Illes, Judika. *The Element Encyclopedia of Witchcraft* (Element, 2005)

Silverwind, Selene. *The Witch's Journal: Charms, Spells, Potions and Enchantments* (Apple Press, 2009)

WEBSITES

HISTORY

exemplore.com/wicca-witchcraft
salemwitchmuseum.com
wiccanspells.info

COVEN INFORMATION

witchescoven.com
witchesofthecraft.com
witchescoven.net

WITCHCRAFT TOOLS AND SUPPLIES

www.13moons.com
www.amazon.com
crystalearthrockshop.com
newmooncottage.com
themagickalcat.com
www.whitemagickalchemy.com/witchcraft-supplies

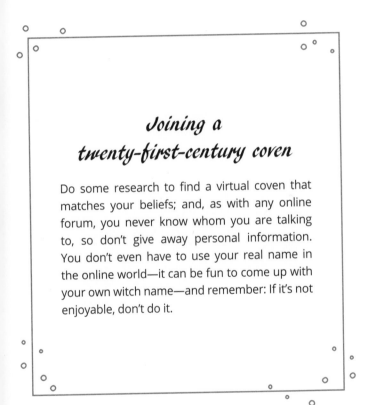

Joining a twenty-first-century coven

Do some research to find a virtual coven that matches your beliefs; and, as with any online forum, you never know whom you are talking to, so don't give away personal information. You don't even have to use your real name in the online world—it can be fun to come up with your own witch name—and remember: If it's not enjoyable, don't do it.

Disclaimer

The primary purpose of this book is to entertain.
The author and publisher shall have neither liability
nor responsibility for loss or damage caused by the
information contained within this book.

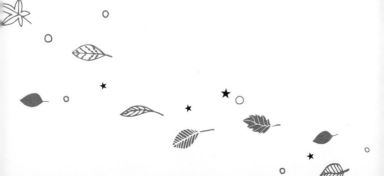

Go and make magic!